From Your Friends At The

NOVEMBER

A MONTH OF REPRODUCIBLES AT YOUR FINGERTIPS!

Grade 1

Editor:
Susan Hohbach Walker

Writers:
Catherine Broome, Lisa Buchholz,
Amy Harders, Lucia Kemp Henry, Cynthia Holcomb,
Mary Lester, Sharon Murphy, Mary Rosenberg

Art Coordinator:
Clevell Harris

Artists:
Jennifer Tipton Bennett, Pam Crane,
Nick Greenwood, Clevell Harris, Susan Hodnett,
Sheila Krill, Rob Mayworth, Barry Slate

Cover Artist:
Jennifer Tipton Bennett

www.themailbox.com

©1999 by THE EDUCATION CENTER, INC.
All rights reserved.
ISBN #1-56234-262-2

Manufactured in the United States

10 9 8 7 6 5 4 3

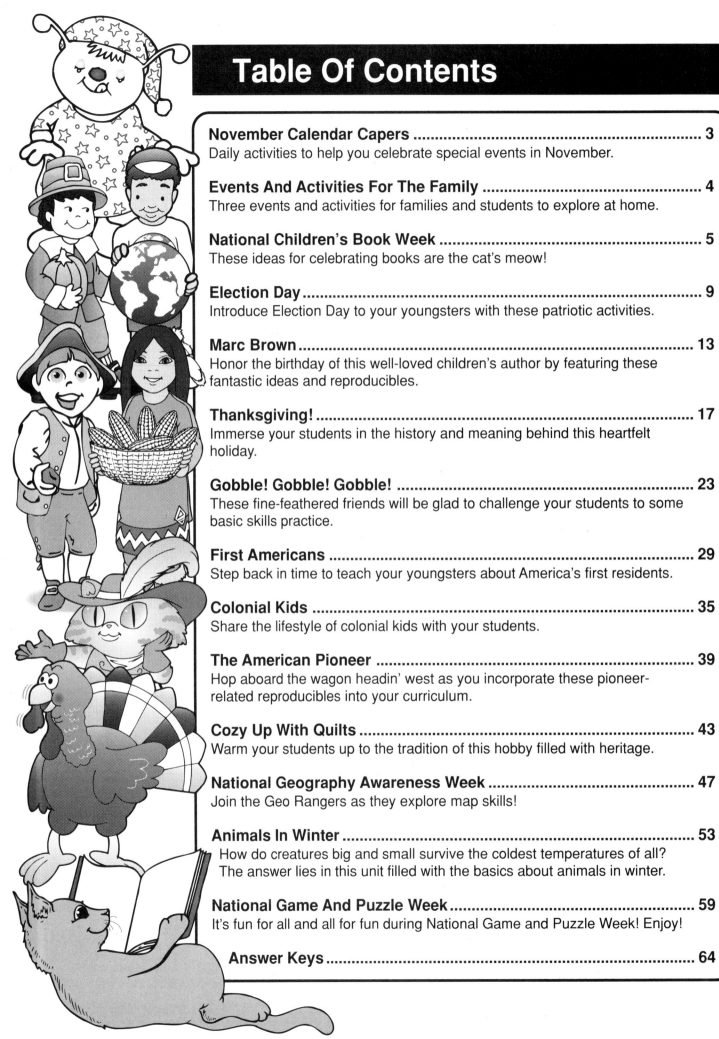

Table Of Contents

November Calendar Capers

Monday	Tuesday	Wednesday	Thursday	Friday
National Authors' Day is November 1. Have each student share a story by his favorite author. 	November 3 is Sandwich Day. Challenge students to list the steps involved in making a peanut-butter sandwich. Write the steps on the chalkboard.	Cat Week begins the first Sunday in November. Invite students who have pet cats to bring pictures of them to class.	The first automobile show was held November 3, 1900. To commemorate this special event, have each child draw a picture or make a clay model of a car.	James Naismith, the inventor of the game of basketball, was born on November 6, 1861. Have students list as many words that have *ball* in them as possible.
Celebrate Lois Ehlert's November 9 birthday by sharing *Red Leaf, Yellow Leaf* (Harcourt Brace Jovanovich, Publishers; 1991). Have students make their own collages like those in the book. 	Challenge students to write poems about the month of November. Encourage students to begin their poems "November is the time when…" *November*	November 11 is Veterans Day. Invite a local veteran to visit your classroom to talk about his experiences while in the armed services.	Robert Louis Stevenson, author of *Treasure Island*, was born on November 13, 1850. Have each student draw a map of an island and then mark spots for trees, rivers, caves, and a treasure. 	William Steig's birthday is November 14. Read aloud *Sylvester And The Magic Pebble* (Atheneum Books For Young Readers, 1995). Ask each child what she would wish for if she had a magic pebble.
Artist Georgia O'Keeffe was born on November 15, 1887. She is known for her paintings of nature and of the American Southwest. Have each student paint a desert scene. 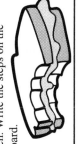	Celebrate International Drum Month by reading aloud *Max Found Two Sticks* (Simon & Schuster Books For Young Readers, 1994) by Brian Pinkney.	November 18 is Mickey Mouse's birthday. On this day in 1928, he first appeared on the screen in *Steamboat Willie*. Have each student draw a picture of and name her own cartoon mouse.	November is Aviation History Month. Have each student keep a tally of how many airplanes he sees or hears today.	National Clean Out Your Refrigerator Day is November 20. Ask students to name other things that have to be cleaned out regularly.
November 21 is World Hello Day. Ask students to greet as many schoolmates as possible throughout the day. 	National Game And Puzzle Week is observed annually the last week in November. Invite students to bring games or puzzles to school to share with their classmates during free time.	Ask each student to list ten things for which she is thankful.	Have students plan a Thanksgiving Day meal for their families.	Thanksgiving was named a holiday because of a presidential proclamation. Have students brainstorm new holidays they think the president should create. 

©1999 The Education Center, Inc. • *November Monthly Reproducibles* • Grade 1 • TEC964

3

November
Events And Activities For The Family

Directions: Select at least one activity below to complete as a family by the end of November.
(Challenge: See if your family can complete all three activities.)

"Leaf" The Decorating To Us!

Bring a touch of autumn to your dinner table with place cards created for your family. Have your youngster collect a few leaves of varying sizes and shapes. Then have him or her lay a sheet of white paper on top of a leaf and color wide, quick strokes over it with a crayon. Next help your child cut out the resulting leaf rubbing. Repeat this process until there are two leaves for each place card. Then have your youngster fold a large index card in half lengthwise. Glue one or two leaf rubbings onto each card, and write the name of a family member with a marker or crayon. Put the appropriate place card by each plate. What a lovely fall display!

Cassidy

Happy Birthday, Kevin Henkes!

November 27 is author and illustrator Kevin Henkes' birthday. Henkes has written more than 20 children's books and novels and has won several awards. Meet his lovable characters Lilly, Owen, and Chester by sharing the following books with your youngsters:
Julius, The Baby Of The World (Greenwillow Books, 1990)
Lilly's Purple Plastic Purse (Greenwillow Books, 1996)
Chester's Way (Greenwillow Books, 1988)
Owen (Greenwillow Books, 1993)

Aboard The *Mayflower*

Include this entertaining oral memory game in your family's Thanksgiving celebration. Begin the game with the story starter, "We're Pilgrims aboard the *Mayflower*. When we get to America, I hope we see one…" Then name an item and make a motion, such as patting the head or blinking. The next family member repeats the same phrase and motion, and then adds "two [a different item]" and a different motion. The next family member continues the pattern. A player is "out" if he is unable to accurately remember all of the items and motions in the correct sequence. Declare the last remaining player the winner. Now, that's a memorable way to reinforce sequencing skills!

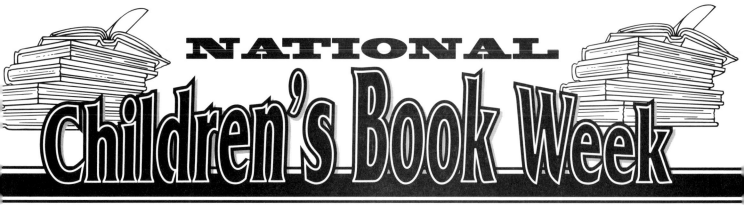

NATIONAL Children's Book Week

Curl up with a good book to celebrate National Children's Book Week, celebrated annually during the week before Thanksgiving. Children can't help but love a good book, and the following activities will only enhance their appreciation.

A "Purr-fect" Bookmark

Help each student create a unique bookmark to accompany her favorite books! Give each child a copy of the bookmark and book patterns on page 6 and have her cut them out. Instruct each child to fold the small rectangular book patterns in half on the dotted lines so they resemble books. Have her think of two of her favorite books and write each title on the cover of a book pattern. Encourage students to draw tiny illustrations inside each book pattern and color the bookmark as desired. Finally, have each child place a small amount of glue on each place indicated on the bookmark. Then have her place a folded book pattern (gray side down) atop each glue area. The completed bookmark will be a special reminder to enjoy some favorite stories during National Children's Book Week.

Teacher Trade

Students are always eager to hear a story. Make storytime extraspecial during National Children's Book Week by having a variety of teachers share a favorite story with your youngsters. In advance, ask each of several teachers in your school or department to prepare a special reading of a favorite book. Design a schedule so that teachers exchange classrooms each day during an arranged storytime. (The number of days will vary depending on how many participants you have.) Both teachers and students will enjoy the variety in their routines.

Not Just A Book Report

Your students will enjoy reporting on a story when it means creating this eye-catching display. Give each child a copy of page 8. Have him tell about a book he recently read by drawing or writing to complete each cutout. Prepare a sentence strip for each child by bringing the ends together and stapling it into a ring. Give one stapled strip to each child and have him glue the characters around it as shown. Exhibit these stand-up displays throughout your classroom so each student can enjoy the book reviews.

These Books Are "Purr-fect" For Me!

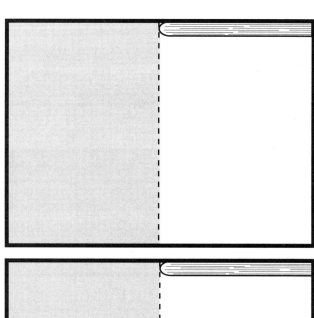

Glue here.

National Children's Book Week

Glue here.

Finished Sample

These Books Are "Purr-fect" For Me!

Arthur's Tooth

National Children's Book Week

Cats

Curled Up With A Good Book

Look at the picture on each book.
Write the missing vowel to complete each title.

One Happy
P__p

My Two
S___cks

The Cat's
B__g

My Green
Fr___g

All About
B__ds

The Red
M___tten

B__gs!

A Big
P__g

B___ts

Who Is In
The B___x?

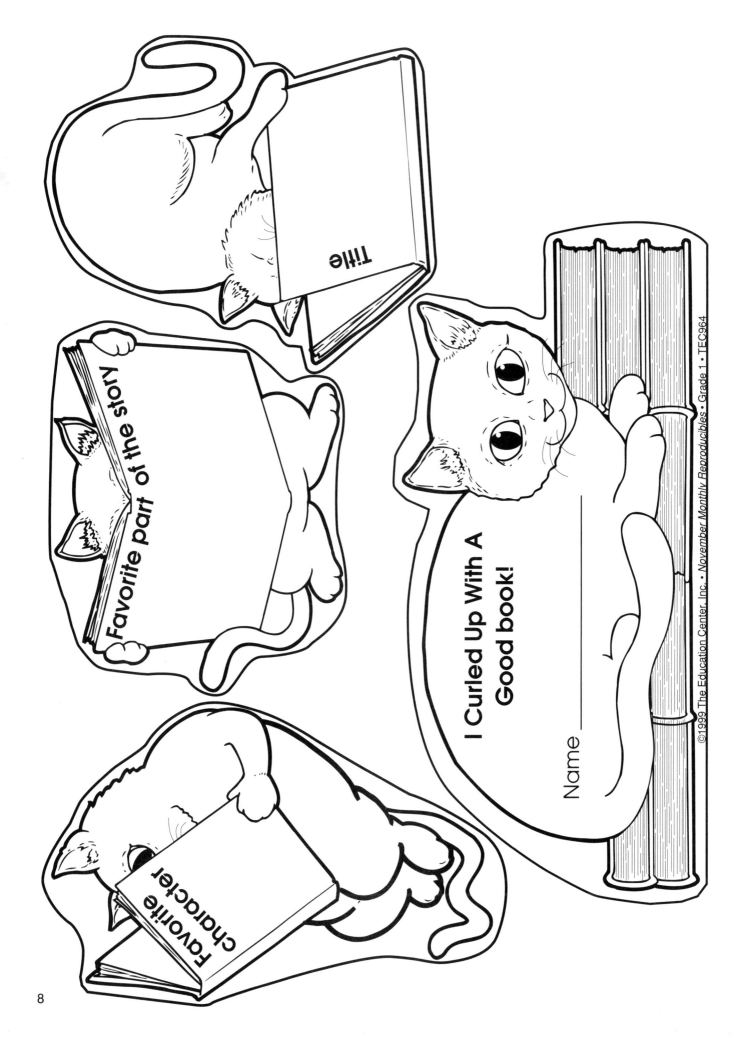

Title

Favorite part of the story

I Curled Up With A Good book!

Name _____

Favorite character

Election Day

It's the first Tuesday after the first Monday in November. What does that mean? On this day, we have the opportunity to make our choices in the voting booth. Reinforce the importance of exercising our patriotic privilege with these voting-related activities and reproducibles.

Cast Your Ballot!

Each year, the American people vote for candidates of their choice to hold various government positions. On Election Day, each voter reports to a polling station to cast her vote on a secret ballot. Introduce the concept of casting a ballot by holding your own class election on a topic of your choice. In advance, make a three-sided cardboard enclosure to fit atop a student desk. Place the desk in the hallway or in a private area in the classroom. Also, program a copy of page 11 to show the topic and choices for the vote; then photocopy a class supply of the ballot. If desired, form small student committees to campaign for each of the choices. When it's time for the vote, call each student one at a time to sit in the "booth" and cast his vote using a copy of the preprogrammed ballot. After he marks his choice, have him place his ballot in a decorated ballot box. Once each child has participated, count the votes and discuss the results.

Don't Forget!

As Election Day draws near, have students encourage their eligible family members to get out and vote! These decorative doorknob signs will provide a patriotic reminder that voting day is fast approaching. To make the project, each student will need crayons, scissors, glue, and a copy of page 12. Instruct him to color the page using red, white, and blue crayons. Next have him cut out the four letters and glue them to the matching shapes on his sign. To finish, have him cut out his sign on the heavy, solid outline, making a slit for the doorknob as indicated. Have students take their signs home a few days prior to Election Day to remind their parents to get to the polls!

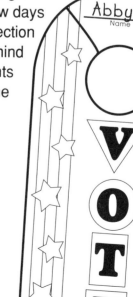

9

The Votes Are In!

Count the votes in each box.
Write the numbers on the lines.
Circle the bigger number in each box.

Ballot Box

Vote For Your Favorite Pet

_____   _____

Vote For Your Favorite Food

_____   _____

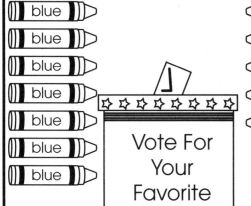

Vote For Your Favorite Color

_____   _____

Vote For Your Favorite Season

_____   _____

Vote For Your Favorite Treat

_____   _____

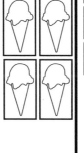

Vote For Your Favorite Sport

_____   _____

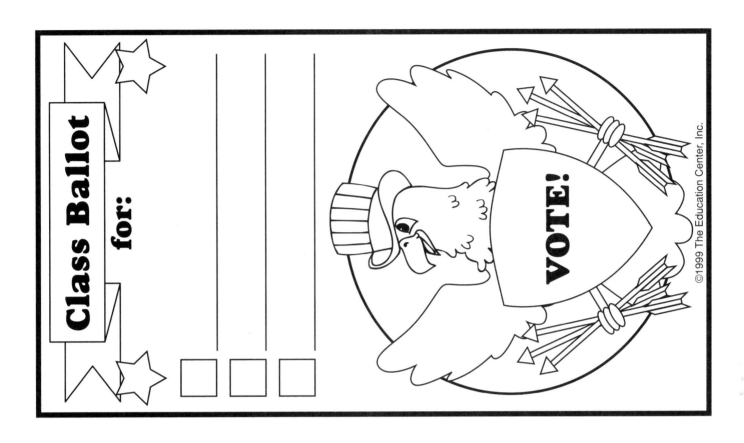

Class Ballot

for:

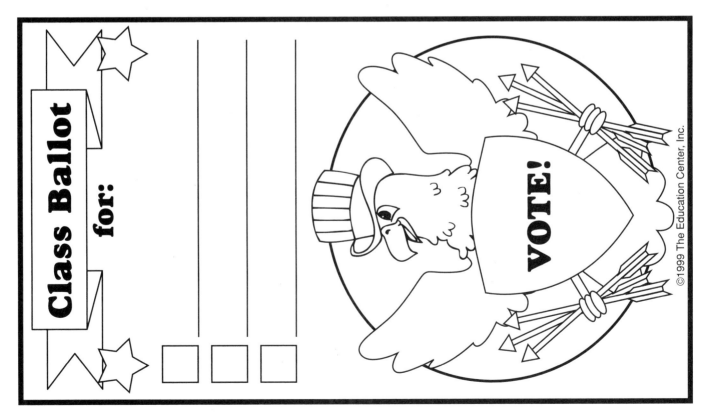

Class Ballot

for:

©1999 The Education Center, Inc.

Election Day Doorknob Sign

Let's Vote!

Election Day is the first Tuesday in November.
Make a sign that reminds people to vote.
Follow your teacher's directions.

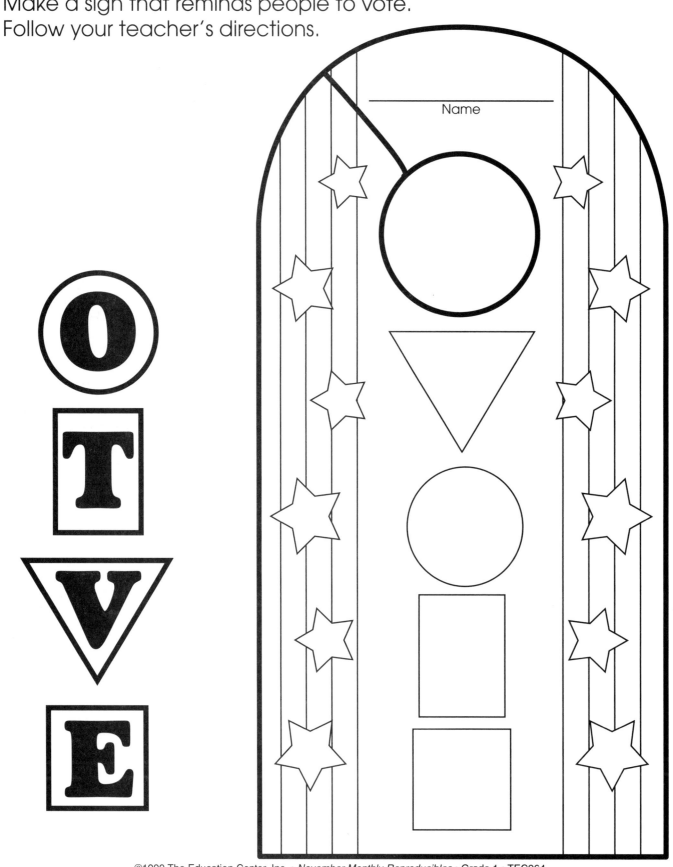

Name

MARC BROWN

Feature the talents of Marc Brown during a special celebration in honor of his birthday on November 25. This popular children's book author and illustrator has likely won your students' hearts through his popular book series based on Arthur the aardvark.

A Bit About Brown

Like many children, Marc Brown enjoyed drawing as a child. Marc's ability was praised and supported by his grandmother, who also passed on her storytelling talent to him. He took his talent a step farther by attending the Cleveland Art Institute. But Marc didn't always make a living telling stories or drawing. He found himself in roles such as truck driver, chef, and college professor to support his family. His own children were an inspiration to his work as an author. In fact, the character, Arthur, was created during the telling of a bedtime tale to his first son. If you look closely, you'll find that Marc hid the names of his sons, Tolon and Tucker, in the illustrations of all but one of his Arthur books. His daughter's name, Eliza, appears in all the Arthur books that have been published since 1986.

Postcards To Pals

Friends are bound to miss one another when they're apart. And missing his best friend, Buster, is exactly what happens to Arthur when he takes a vacation with his family. Share the story, *Arthur's Family Vacation* (Little, Brown And Company; 1993), with your students; then ask them to recall the postcard that Arthur wrote and mailed to Buster. Give your students the opportunity to create a postcard for a special friend. Distribute a white construction-paper copy of page 14 to each child. Have her cut out the card along the heavy solid outline. Then ask her to think of a school friend. Encourage her to write a special message to that person and address the card as directed. Finally, ask each child to turn the card over and decorate it with a colorful drawing. If possible, deliver each child's card to the designated recipient.

Hi, __Buster__,
I sure miss you! Wish you were in my class. We could have so much fun.

Your friend,
__Arthur__
(my name)

To: __Buster__
(friend's name)
__Laughlin Primary__
(name of school)
__100__
(room number)

To:

_____
(friend's name)

_____
(name of school)

_____
(room number)

Hi, _____,

_____

_____

_____

_____

Your friend,

_____
(my name)

Note To The Teacher: Use with "Postcards To Pals" on page 13.

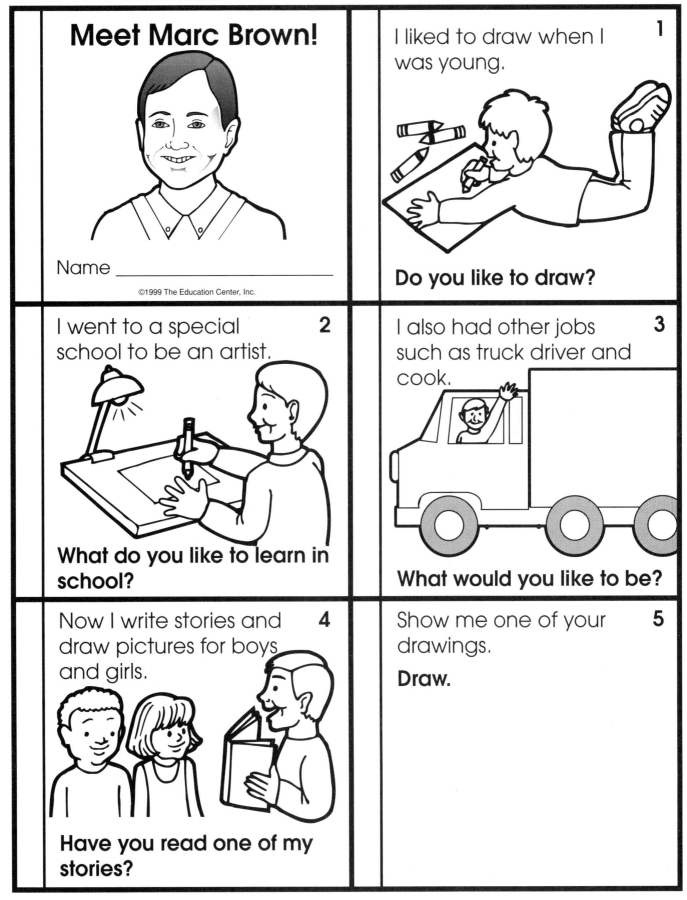

Meet Marc Brown!

Name _____

©1999 The Education Center, Inc.

1

I liked to draw when I was young.

Do you like to draw?

2

I went to a special school to be an artist.

What do you like to learn in school?

3

I also had other jobs such as truck driver and cook.

What would you like to be?

4

Now I write stories and draw pictures for boys and girls.

Have you read one of my stories?

5

Show me one of your drawings.

Draw.

©1999 The Education Center, Inc. • *November Monthly Reproducibles* • Grade 1 • TEC964

Note To The Teacher: Review "A Bit About Brown" on page 13. Then have each child color, cut out, sequence, and staple these booklet pages.

Name_____

Trouble On The Set

Draw one thing that gave Arthur trouble during play practice.

Note To The Teacher: Read aloud Marc Brown's *Arthur's Thanksgiving* (Little, Brown And Company; 1983). Then have each child refer to the story to complete this page.

THANKSGIVING!

Most Americans think of the first Thanksgiving as being the one that took place at Plymouth Colony in October 1621. Today Thanksgiving is celebrated on the fourth Thursday in November. For Americans this holiday commemorates a small group of colonists who journeyed across the Atlantic so they could worship as they pleased. It is a time to give thanks not only for nature's bounty, but also for freedom.

Thinking About Thanksgiving

Introduce your study of the first Thanksgiving with a chart to capture students' interest. Before the lesson, visually divide a large sheet of bulletin-board paper into three sections. Label each section as shown. Begin your unit by inviting children to contribute information they already know about the Pilgrims. Record these facts in the first section of your chart. Next have students generate questions they have about the Pilgrims. Record the questions in the middle section and use this information to help direct your study. Then, as you continue your unit, take time after each lesson to have students summarize new facts they have learned while you write the information in the last section of the chart. By the end of the unit, your students will have a written record of all they have learned.

The Pilgrims

What We Know	What We Want To Know	What We've Learned
They were on a ship. They had the first Thanksgiving. The Indians helped them.	Why did they come to America? Did children come, too?	

What A Journey!

The Pilgrims had many hardships on their voyage to America. With over 100 people on board the *Mayflower,* there was not much space on the ship. The crowded journey took 66 days, and the food supply was limited to items that would not spoil during the trip. To give your students a feel for what the journey was like, tape off a section on the floor and have them sit very close together inside the area while you read a story, such as *If You Sailed On The Mayflower In 1620* by Ann McGovern (Scholastic Inc., 1993). Then serve them a meal fit for a seaworthy Pilgrim by giving each child a soda cracker, a small piece of beef jerky, a wedge of cheese, and a small cup of water. Ask students to imagine the Pilgrims enduring similar meals and crowded conditions for over two months! To conclude the lesson, have students return to their desks and volunteer information to add to the chart described in "Thinking About Thanksgiving" on this page.

Name_____

Thankful Thoughts

What were the pilgrims thankful for?
Read.
Cut and glue.

©1999 The Education Center, Inc. • *November Monthly Reproducibles* • Grade 1 • TEC964

The corn grew.	Many houses were built.
They were feeling well.	The Indians were their friends.
A ship came to get them.	They could worship.

Pilgrim Pie

Say each picture name.
Circle the vowel.
Color each box by the code.

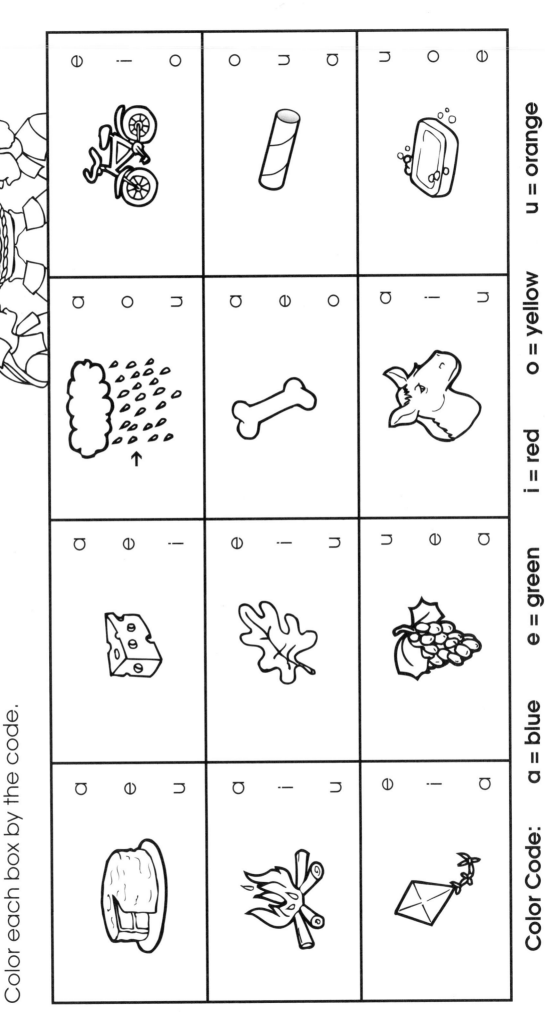

Color Code: a = blue   e = green   i = red   o = yellow   u = orange

Thanksgiving!
Short vowels

Feasting Friends

Color the pictures in each row
that have the vowel sound shown.

ă				
ĕ				
ĭ	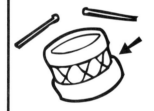			
ŏ	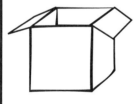			
ŭ				

Name_____

Horn Of Plenty

Count the pieces of fruit.
Write the number of pieces.
Add.

1.

_____ + _____ = _____

2.

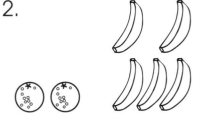

_____ + _____ = _____

3.

_____ + _____ = _____

4.

_____ + _____ = _____

5.

_____ + _____ = _____

6.

_____ + _____ = _____

7.

_____ + _____ = _____

8.

_____ + _____ = _____

Name_____

Pilgrim Pockets

Count the coins in each pocket.
Circle the correct amount.

16¢   12¢

22¢   13¢

18¢   24¢

23¢   25¢

20¢   15¢

12¢   17¢

13¢   9¢

24¢   21¢

GOBBLE! GOBBLE! GOBBLE!

What bird comes to mind when you think of Thanksgiving? That's right, the turkey! Instead of making plans to cook this fine fowl, turn him into the center of attention with these basic skill review pages.

Turkeys By The Tens

Combine a great turkey craft with skip-counting practice, and you'll have turkeys by the tens! Give each child a six-inch paper plate, a brad, and a white construction-paper copy of page 26. Also provide a work area supplied with brown paint and brushes for students to share. To create a turkey, have each child paint the bottom of her paper plate brown. Next have each child color the feather, head, and leg pieces (on page 26) as desired, and cut out each piece along the bold cutting line. When the paint has dried, ask each child to put the feathers in order by tens around the top of the plate. Check each child's work for accuracy before having her glue the feathers to the plate. Finally, have her insert a brad through the • on the turkey's neck and then through the center of the plate. Then, have each child glue the feet to the plate as shown. To review counting by tens, have each child move the turkey's head so that the beak points to each number as she counts aloud. Now that's an activity your students will gobble up!

Turkey Talk!

Imagine waking up on a Saturday morning, opening your mouth to speak, and having "Gobble! Gobble!" come out! Present this scene to your students; then ask each child to think about what his day would be like if he could utter only turkey talk. How would he get through his day? How would he communicate with his family? How does it make him feel? Give each child some time to think or talk about his day of turkey talk; then give him a copy of page 27. Ask each child to write about his day of turkey talk. You may find your little gobblers to be quite resourceful under the strange circumstances.

Gobbler Groupings

Each turkey has ten feathers.
How many feathers are in each group?
Count by tens. Cut and glue.

Bonus Box: On the back of this sheet, write the tens from 10 to 100.

1 ten = 10 feathers	2 tens = 20 feathers
3 tens = 30 feathers	4 tens = 40 feathers
5 tens = 50 feathers	6 tens = 60 feathers
7 tens = 70 feathers	8 tens = 80 feathers
9 tens = 90 feathers	

Turkey Mix-Up

Tom turkey is cooking dinner.
His food got all mixed up!
Help him sort long vowels
from short vowels.

Remember!
Long vowels say
their names.

Cut and glue.

short vowels	long vowels

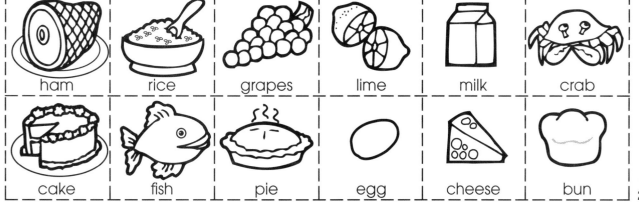

ham	rice	grapes	lime	milk	crab
cake	fish	pie	egg	cheese	bun

25

Turkey Pattern

40

30 Glue.

Glue.

80

20 Glue.

Glue.

100

60 Glue.

Glue.

10

70 Glue.

Glue.

50

06 Glue.

Glue.

Glue.

Note To The Teacher: Use with "Turkeys By The Tens" on page 23.

Name _____

Turkey Talk!

Note To The Teacher: Use with "Turkey Talk!" on page 23.

Name _____

Turkey Time

Color the box that shows the time.

| 2:00 | 11:00 | | 3:00 | 6:00 | | 4:00 | 9:00 | | 5:00 | 12:00 |

| 8:00 | 1:00 | | 7:00 | 3:00 | | 4:00 | 10:00 | | 4:00 | 8:00 |

| 10:00 | 9:00 | | 12:00 | 11:00 | | 7:00 | 2:00 | | 1:00 | 6:00 |

FIRST AMERICANS

Long before the Pilgrims, the colonists, or the pioneers, the Native Americans made their homes on the land we now call America. Use the ideas and reproducibles in this unit to share with your students the rich culture of our first settlers.

Many Different Homes

The first Americans made their homes in many different regions across what is now the United States. Their lifestyles were formed by their surroundings. Share with your students information about Native Americans from four major regions. Then divide the class into four groups and assign each a different region. Provide materials for each group to make a mural showing the people of their region.

The Coastal tribes lived in the forest region between the Pacific Ocean and the Rocky Mountains. The rivers were full of fish to eat, and the cedar trees supplied materials for their homes, canoes, and clothing. Recommended reading: *Totem Pole* by Diane Hoyt-Goldsmith (Holiday House, Inc.; 1994)

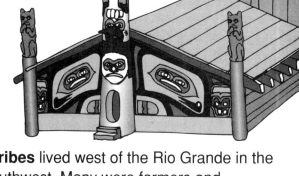

The Desert tribes lived west of the Rio Grande in the dry, rocky Southwest. Many were farmers and depended on corn crops. Some of their homes were made from a clay mixture called *adobe.* Sheep supplied them with both food and clothing. Recommended reading: *Annie And The Old One* by Miska Miles (Little, Brown And Company; 1985)

The Plains tribes settled between the Rocky Mountains and the Mississippi River. They often followed the buffalo, which they depended on for food, clothing, shelter, and tools. They lived in *tipis,* temporary homes made from buffalo hides. Recommended reading: *Iktomi And The Boulder* by Paul Goble (Orchard Books, 1991)

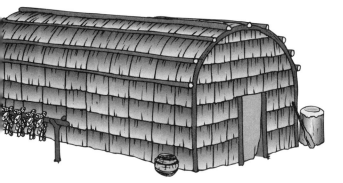

The Woodland tribes lived between the Mississippi River and the East Coast. Depending on the trees in their area, they lived in single-family wigwams or multi-family longhouses. Forest animals were a handy source of meat and clothing. Recommended reading: *The Rough-Face Girl* by Rafe Martin (Paper Star, 1998)

A Special Pocket

As you continue your study of the first Americans, your students will be eager to learn about Native American clothing. If possible share pictures or examples of Native American–style clothing. Point out that although clothing differed from region to region, there was one thing it had in common—no pockets! To carry special items, many tribes would use leather bags or pouches. Some bags were adorned with beadwork designs.

Reinforce this concept by having each student make her own special pocket. For this project, each student will need markers, scissors, glue, a two-foot length of yarn, and a copy of page 31. Instruct her to color the design to resemble beads. Next have her place a small drop of glue atop each bead so that it will appear raised. Allow the glue to dry; then have her cut out the pouch on the heavy solid outline. Instruct her to make fringe by cutting on the broken lines. Have her fold along the center line and glue the bottom (just above the fringe) and sides together, leaving the top open. To complete the pouch, punch a hole on either side of the bag and tie the yarn for a strap. For an added touch, give each student a special treat to carry in her pouch throughout the day.

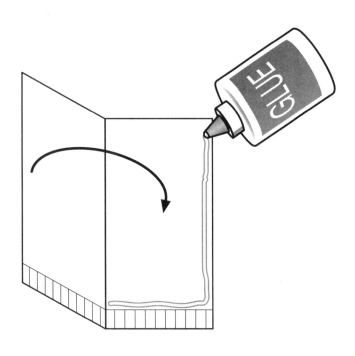

Name_____

A Special Pocket

The Native Americans did not have pockets.
They used special bags to hold small things.

Listen and do.

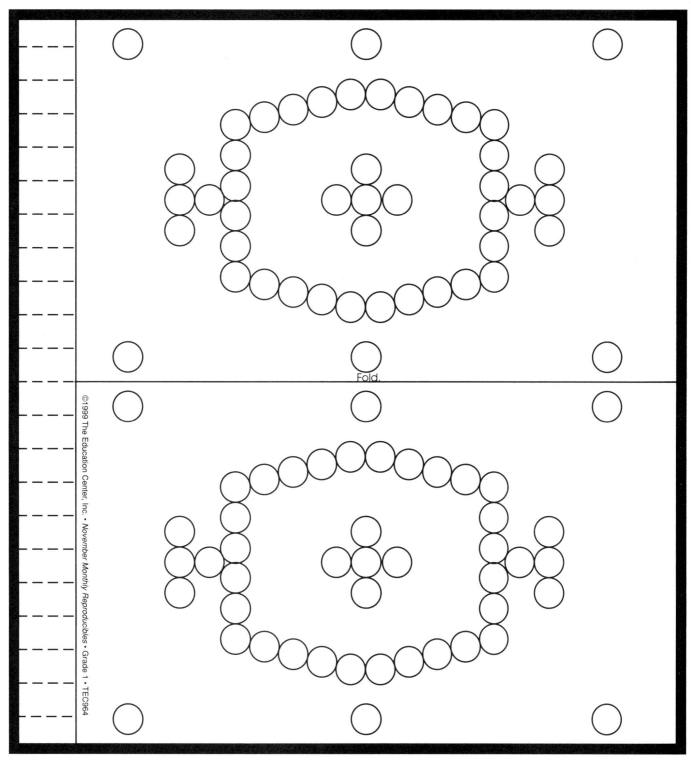

Fold.

©1999 The Education Center, Inc. • November Monthly Reproducibles • Grade 1 • TEC964

Name_____

A Happy Harvest

Subtract.
Cross out foods in each basket to solve.
Write.

8 – 2 = _____

7 – 4 = _____

6 – 3 = _____

5 – 3 = _____

8 – 5 = _____

5 – 4 = _____

6 – 2 = _____

7 – 6 = _____

8 – 6 = _____

6 – 4 = _____

Bonus Box: There were 8 apples in the basket. Sam used 3 apples to make a pie. How many apples were left in the basket?

©1999 The Education Center, Inc. • *November Monthly Reproducibles* • Grade 1 • TEC964 • Key p. 64

Name_____

Tall Totem Poles

Some Native Americans made totem poles.
Some totem poles were very tall!
They used symbols to show animals on the poles.
Cut out the animal symbols.
Glue in ABC order.

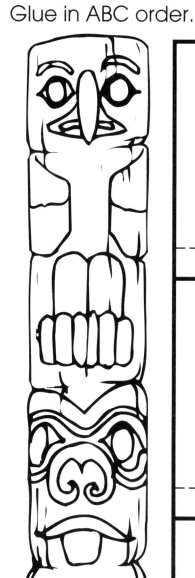

Bear

Glue.

Whale

Glue.

Eagle

Glue.

Snake

Glue.

Owl

Glue.

Frog

Glue.

Note To The Teacher: Have each child glue the squares together so that the animal names are in ABC order from top to bottom.

Beautiful Beadwork

Many Native Americans made designs with beads.
Sometimes they made patterns.
Draw to finish each pattern.

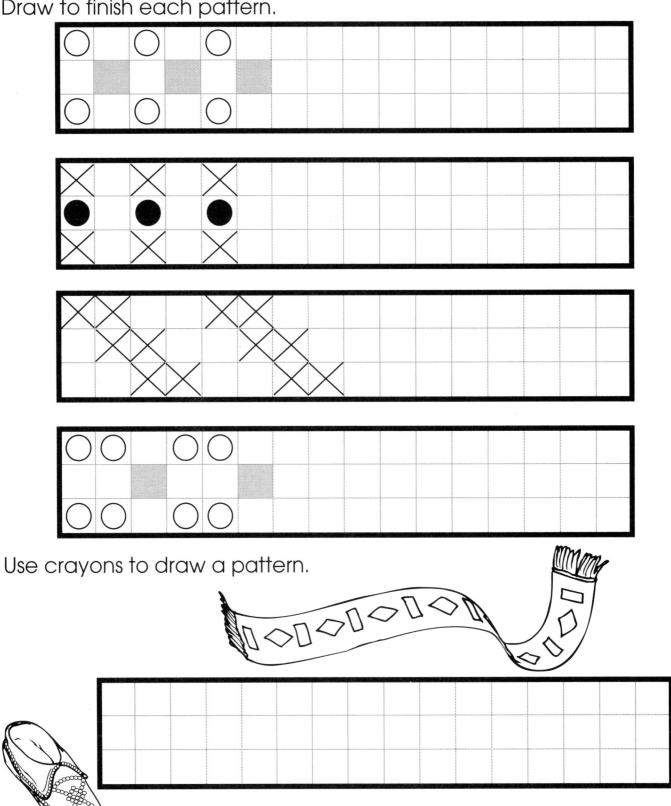

Use crayons to draw a pattern.

©1999 The Education Center, Inc. • *November Monthly Reproducibles* • Grade 1 • TEC964

Colonial Kids

Between the late 1500s and the late 1700s, many European settlers were attracted to the New World for a variety of reasons. Some were in search of political and religious freedom, whereas others hoped to gain better economic opportunities. With them came their children, who saw the land we call America through young eyes. Give your students a glimpse of life as a colonial kid by sharing these activities and reproducibles.

Dressing The Part

Colonial children were very different from modern-day children in many ways, and their clothing was no exception. Share some of the clothing facts from this page with your students. Then give a white construction-paper copy of page 37 to each child. Instruct each child to cut out the body pattern and draw or color the face to resemble his own. (If desired, provide a photograph of each child to cut out and glue onto the face of the pattern.) Then have him color, cut out, and glue the appropriate clothing to the body pattern. Now each child can visualize what he might have looked like had he lived in colonial days.

Most colonists made their own clothing. Children were often trained to help make the cloth. In fact, the Massachusetts Colony even passed a law stating that all children must learn to spin wool and flax.

A "pudding" was a thickly padded cap worn by a baby as she began walking. This protected the baby's head in case of a fall.

At age five or six, colonial children began wearing shoes instead of slippers. By this age they had more chores to do, and shoes provided more protection for their feet.

Most colonial children wore soft leather shoes that were similar to moccasins. Wealthier children wore hard-soled shoes imported from Europe.

At age five or six, colonial boys were "breeched." This means that they began wearing pants instead of long robes and petticoats that both younger boys and girls wore.

A New Twist For An Old Game

Your students will be amazed to know that colonial children played a game we still play today—hopscotch! Add a new twist to this old game by incorporating reading, math, or spelling skill reinforcement to the fun. In advance, use chalk to draw several hopscotch grids on school sidewalks or play areas. Then prepare each grid using one of the ideas listed at the right. Send a small group of students to each hopscotch grid, and encourage them to try the new version of this old favorite.

Programming

— Write an addition or a subtraction problem in each square. As a child hops on each square, he answers the problem. If he's in error, he begins again.
— Write one vocabulary or sight word in each square. As a child hops on each square, she reads the word.
— Write one spelling word in each square. As a student hops on each square, he spells the word.

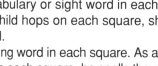

Colonial Hornbook

5 + 4	6 + 3	8 + 2	4 + 3
0 + 7	9 + 1	3 + 7	5 + 2
3 + 2	3 + 6	2 + 8	3 + 4
5 + 5	7 + 2	1 + 9	7 + 3

Bonus Box: Colonial kids used a one-page hornbook to learn their alphabet and numbers. On the back of this sheet, write the alphabet and the numbers 1–10.

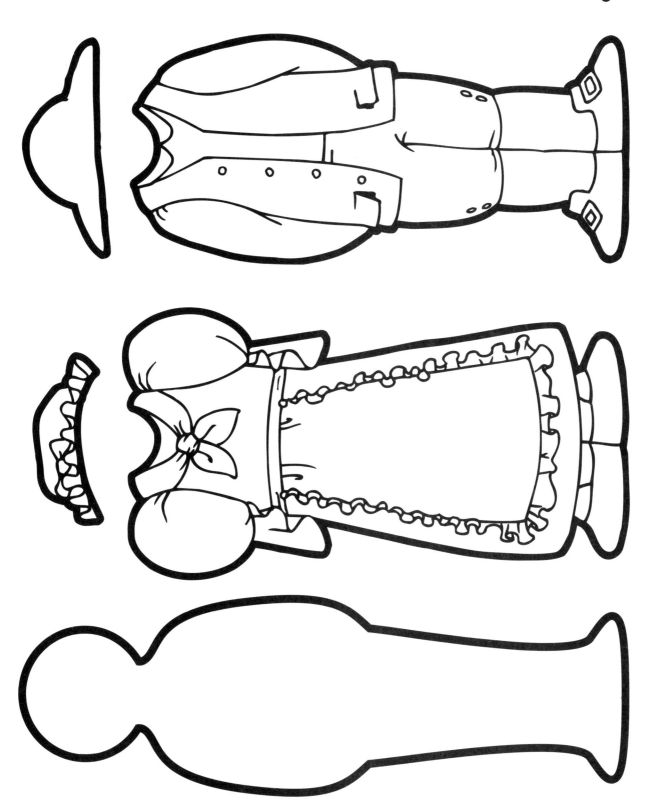

Note To The Teacher: Use with "Dressing The Part" on page 35.

37

Name _____

Colonial Comforts

These are things some colonial kids had in their homes.
Say each picture name.
Cut and glue to match.

bed	doll	pot	dish	mug
chest	log	hat	wig	socks

The American Pioneer

From roughly 1760 to 1850, thousands of people ventured west, moving America's western boundary from the Appalachian Mountains to the Pacific Ocean. These people, known as pioneers, had a variety of reasons for their journeys. Some were in search of a better way of life for their families, and others were looking for an adventure. The pioneers moved westward in two large groups. In the first stage, pioneers from the East Coast and even Europe ventured west to the Mississippi valley. During the second movement, pioneers traveled as far west as California.

Get Shaking!

Busy pioneer families had an interesting way of making butter while on the move! They hung a leather bag full of cream from the back of their wagon, and the rough ride churned the cream to butter while they traveled. Your students can experience this firsthand with just a pint of heavy cream and a jar! Pour the cream into a jar (larger than one pint) and seal tightly. Then get shaking! Have each child shake the jar for a short time before passing it to another student. After approximately ten minutes of shaking, the cream will solidify into soft butter. Serve this creamy spread on crackers or bread for all your students to enjoy.

Pioneer Predictions

The American pioneers didn't have elaborate methods or tools for predicting the weather. Instead, they observed nature for signs of the weather conditions to come. Use the lists on this page to review some pioneer weather indicators with your students. Then have each child in your class give his predicting skills a try. On an assigned morning, ask a student to predict the weather for that day. Ask him to share with the class his reasons for his forecast. Record the prediction, and revisit it at the end of the day to discuss the actual weather. Each child will enjoy this challenge and who knows, he may think of a more accurate weather indicator than the meteorologist!

Pioneer Good-Weather Signs
birds flying high
clouds high in the sky
lots of dew at night
loudly singing cicadas (insects)
smoke rising quickly

Pioneer Weather-Warning Signs
dark or overcast clouds
a halo around the sun
smoke curling downward

A Full Load

Cut. Glue each picture next to its beginning blend.

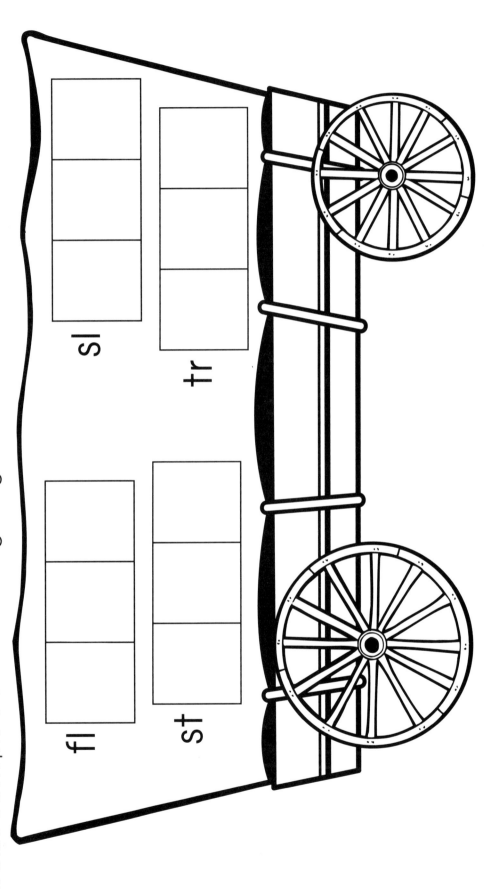

fl

sl

st

tr

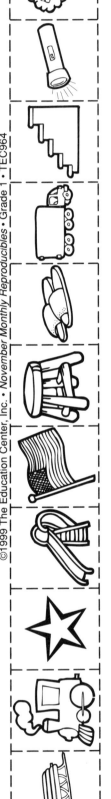

Name _____

The American Pioneer
Vocabulary

A Pioneer Picture Story

These pioneers rode in a  on their trip west.

The wagon was pulled by .

They loaded the wagon with .

They also brought .

They drove through tall  and over .

Sometimes the pioneers were . It was hard work to go so far.

When they got to their new home they built a .

©1999 The Education Center, Inc. • November Monthly Reproducibles • Grade 1 • TEC964 • Key p. 64

 wagon

food

 sad

mountains

house

furniture

grass

 pizza

 oxen

 boat

41

Name _____

A Different Way Of Life

Cut and glue to match each pair.

Things sure have changed!

then now

then now

then now

then now

Cozy Up With Quilts

Settle in and spend some time exploring one of the world's coziest creations: quilts. Quilting actually began in prehistoric times. The tradition was later brought to the United States by the colonists, who practiced quilting skills they had learned in Europe. Colonial women often held *quilting bees* as social gatherings. Today, these colorful creations are not only used to stay warm, but are also recognized as a form of art.

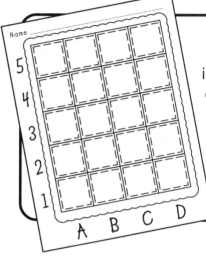

Quilting Coordinates

Help your students piece together beginning map skills and listening skills with this coordinate challenge. In preparation, create a quilting pattern similar to the one shown and give each child a copy. Then provide oral directions for your students to decorate their quilt. For example, you might say, "Find A3. Draw a yellow sun in A3." Continue giving directions until a desired number of squares have been decorated. No doubt your students will be proud of their listening skills and their beautifully designed quilts!

Crazy Quilt!

Watch out! Your students will be crazy about this inventive game! In advance, create a patchwork gameboard by gluing sheets of construction paper (in about five different colors) to a piece of bulletin-board paper. (If desired, sew large squares of fabric together to create a more realistic gameboard.) Place it on the floor and have your students stand around it. Give one child a beanbag and ask him to toss it onto a square. After it lands, have him determine a simple action to accompany that color or fabric design. For example, he may bend and touch his toes. Then have everyone repeat the action together. Each time a beanbag lands on that color, the group must repeat that action. Pass the beanbag to the next child. If it lands on a color without an established action, he may decide what the action will be. Continue playing until each child has had a chance to toss the beanbag. This game is especially fun because a new set of actions will be created each time it's played. Your students will love the endless variety!

Cuddly Counting

Count the stars in the boxes.
Write the numbers by fives to 100.

Name_____

Cozy Calculations

Subtract.
Color by the code.

10 − 8	8 − 5	10 − 4	9 − 4
7 − 6	9 − 5	10 − 5	8 − 4
7 − 5	9 − 3	8 − 6	10 − 7
7 − 4	10 − 6	9 − 7	8 − 7

Color Code:

1 = yellow   4 = orange
2 = red   5 = purple
3 = blue   6 = green

Quilt Squares

Say each picture name.
Cut and glue below the matching vowel.

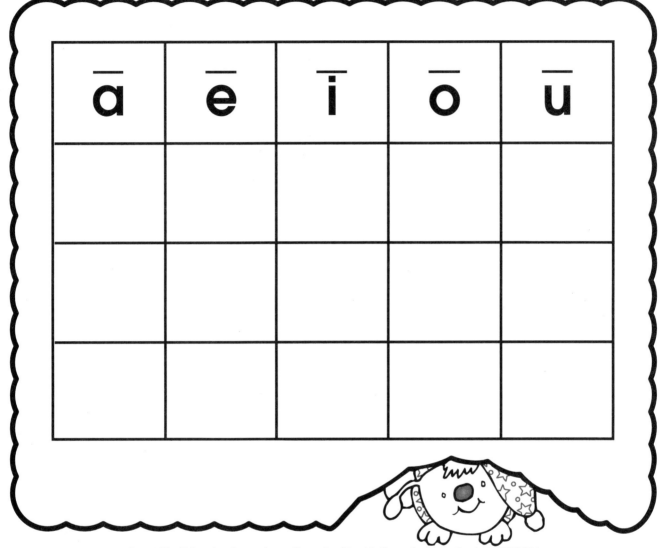

National Geography Awareness Week

There's no better time for a journey with maps than during National Geography Awareness Week, celebrated the third full week in November. So join our Geo Rangers in a fun-filled adventure that's sure to enhance your youngsters' map skills!

Block Party

The transition between the concrete and the abstract can make learning map skills a challenge for first graders. Guide your students' understanding with this activity. Visit your local hardware store to gather a collection of small wooden block remnants. (Be sure they have no rough edges.) Set up a work area with paints and brushes, and encourage your students to paint the blocks to resemble buildings, bridges, cars, and other things found in a town. Place a large piece of bulletin-board paper on the floor and assist your students in creating a miniature town. Encourage them to draw roads, lakes, and landmarks. Have them add the blocks to the town where appropriate. After the model is complete, have each child stand next to the town and look down on it for a bird's-eye view. Next, create a map of the model town on a sheet of poster board. Label the map with the cardinal directions north, south, east, and west. Encourage students to suggest symbols for the various items; then have them coach you as you draw the items on the map. Your students will take great interest in learning to use a map they helped create, and you will find that you can use this valuable tool again and again to reinforce geography skills.

The Geo Rangers

The Geo Rangers are going hiking! But first they must learn some map skills so they won't get lost. Use pages 48–52 to help reinforce map skills, such as using cardinal directions, map symbols, and a map key. After each child completes the activities on pages 49–52, have him cut out each page along the heavy solid lines. Next, have him color a copy of the booklet cover (page 48) and cut it out. Instruct him to sequence the pages behind the booklet cover and staple along the left-hand side to create a ready-to-review geography booklet. If desired, each of the booklet pages can be used independently and do not have to be assembled into a booklet.

Celebrate
National Geography Awareness Week
With The Geo Rangers

Name

The Geo Rangers' Hike

The Geo Rangers are ready to go on a hike.
One ranger brought a **globe** to help them find their way.
The other ranger brought a **map.**

A map is flat and drawn on paper. It can show the whole earth or just part of it.

A globe is shaped like a ball. It shows the whole earth.

globe   **map**

Which will help the Geo Rangers the most? Circle.
Write why you made your choice.

The Geo Rangers Learn About Directional Words

The Geo Rangers are using a map to help them find their way. When they walk toward **N**, they are going *north*. **S** means *south*, **E** means *east*, and **W** means *west*.

Read each set of words.
Draw to finish.

If the rangers walk **west**, they will find....

If they walk **north**, they will find....

If they walk **south**, they will find....

If they walk **east**, they will find....

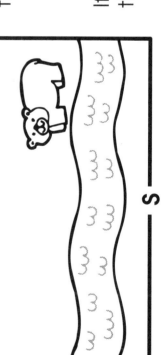

2

The Geo Rangers Learn About Map Symbols

A map is a drawing of a place.
Symbols are used to show things at that place.
A key helps us understand the symbols.

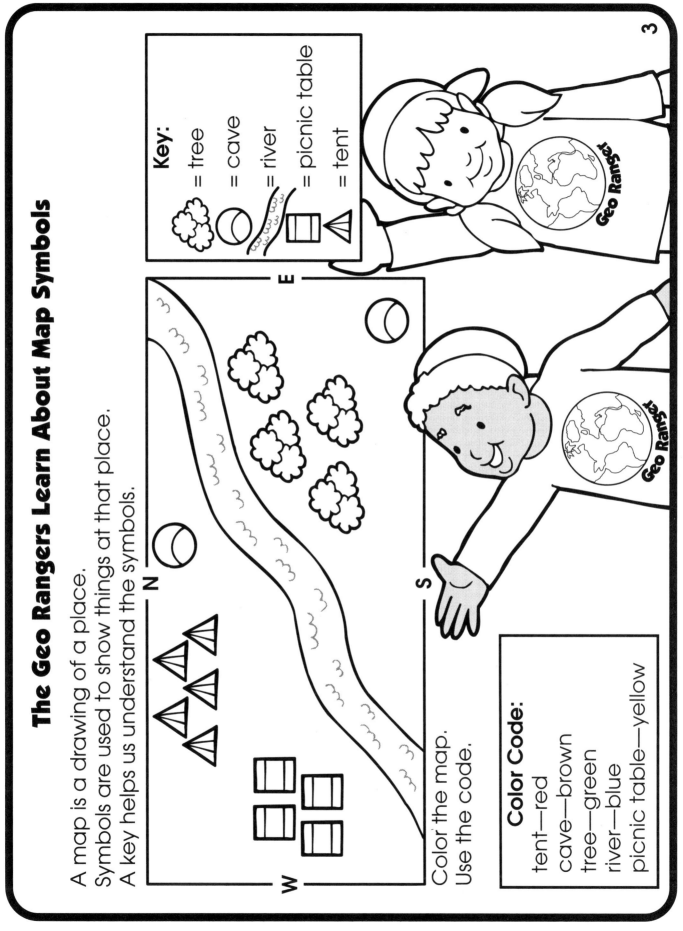

Key:

🌳 = tree
⬤ = cave
〰 = river
▭ = picnic table
△ = tent

Color the map.
Use the code.

Color Code:
tent—red
cave—brown
tree—green
river—blue
picnic table—yellow

The Geo Rangers Use Their Map Skills

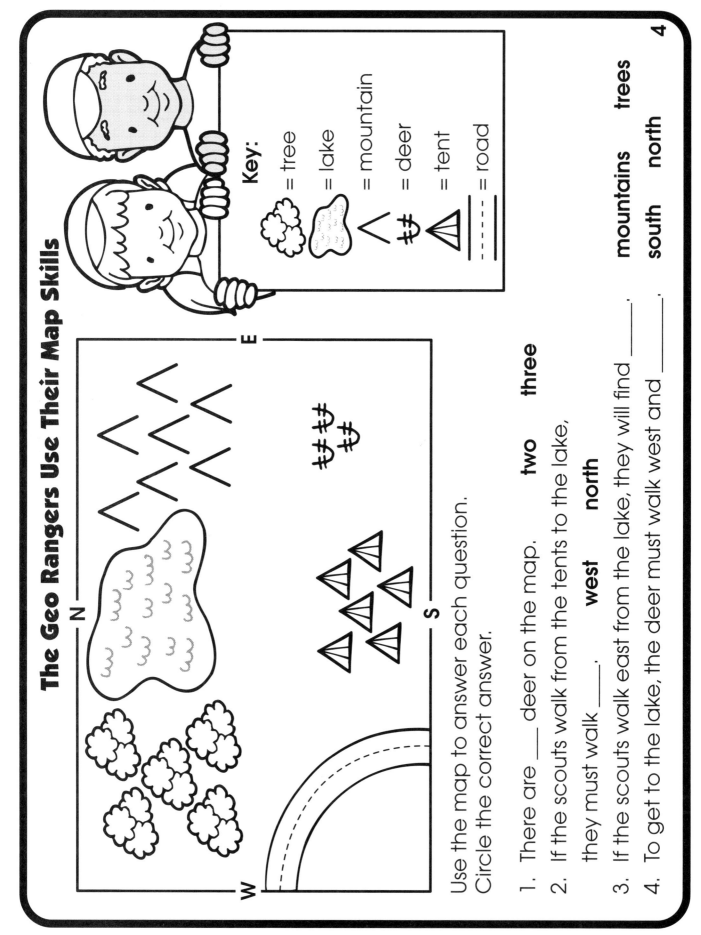

Key:

= tree

= lake

= mountain

= deer

= tent

= road

Use the map to answer each question.
Circle the correct answer.

1. There are ___ deer on the map. **two** **three**

2. If the scouts walk from the tents to the lake,
   they must walk ___. **west** **north**

3. If the scouts walk east from the lake, they will find ___. **mountains** **trees**

4. To get to the lake, the deer must walk west and ___. **south** **north**

Animals In Winter

Whether you're covered in feathers, fur, or skin, you've got to be ready when the chill of winter sets in! When your youngsters study the various ways animals protect themselves against the frigid storms of the season, they will easily see that people use similar ways to keep warm when the weather turns cold.

"Brrr-isk" Winter Booklet

Help your students get ready for winter with a booklet that tells how animals survive the cold weather season. Distribute copies of page 54 and 55 to each child. Have each student complete the cover and five booklet pages using the directions below. Direct each child to cut out and sequence his pages; then staple them together along the left side.

Cover: Decorate the cover by drawing snowflakes, using a snowflake rubber stamp, or adding snowflake stickers for special interest.

Page 1: To make rock shapes, dip your thumb into gray paint; then press prints around the bear to create a rocky cave.

Page 2: Color the nest outline with crayons in fall colors. Glue small pieces of leaves around the squirrel to create a nest.

Page 3: Glue a tiny ball of crumpled white tissue to the rabbit to make a tail. If desired, decorate the snowbank with silver glitter-glue.

Page 4: Color the goose wing brown. Cut a second, similarly shaped wing from brown paper and glue it to the page where indicated.

Page 5: Cut a small semicircle from fabric or felt. Glue it atop the child's head for a hat. Top the hat with a tiny pom-pom. Draw and color facial features.

Animals In Winter
by Danielle

1. Woolly bears hibernate in dens so warm and cozy.

2. Fluffy squirrels sleep in nests curling nose to "toesie."

3. Cuddly rabbits grow thick coats to stay warm in the snow.

4. Feathered geese like it warm, so far off south they go.

5. But when the days are freezing cold, I can't grow fur or fly! So I warmly bundle up and bid the chills good-bye!

Snowy Season Ensembles

Now that you've studied how animals prepare themselves for winter weather, why not help your youngsters focus on the kinds of clothes they'll need to brave the chilly storms of the season? First ask your students what kinds of special clothes people wear to keep warm in the winter; make a list of the suggested items on chart paper. Next, have each child use the clothing suggestions to design and color an ideal winter outfit on a large sheet of white construction paper, embellishing the space around the outfit with snowflake stickers or rubber-stamped snowflake designs. To complete the design ensemble, have each child write or dictate a sentence to explain why her design is especially suited to winter wear. Display your youngsters' seasonal clothing designs and descriptions on a bulletin board titled "Our Special Winter Wear."

Animals In Winter

by _____

1

Woolly bears
hibernate
in dens so warm
and cozy.

2

Fluffy squirrels
sleep in nests
curling nose
to "toesie."

3

Cuddly rabbits
grow thick coats
to stay warm
in the snow.

4

Feathered geese
like it warm,
so far off
south they go.

Glue wing here.

5

But when the days are freezing cold,
I can't grow fur or fly!
So I warmly bundle up
and bid the chills good-bye!

Name _____

Cozy Order

Write the number that comes **before**.
Write the number that comes **after**.

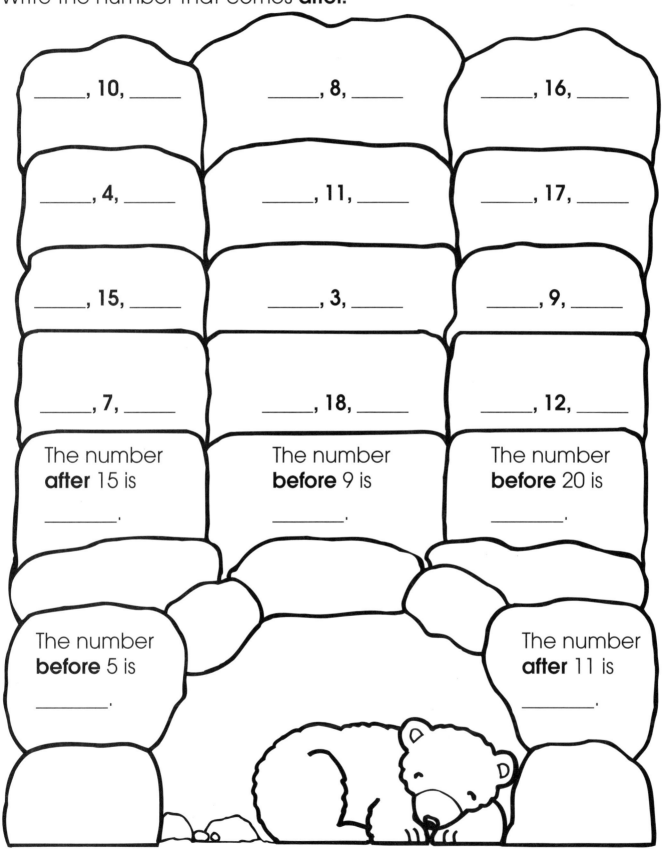

_____ , 10, _____

_____ , 8, _____

_____ , 16, _____

_____ , 4, _____

_____ , 11, _____

_____ , 17, _____

_____ , 15, _____

_____ , 3, _____

_____ , 9, _____

_____ , 7, _____

_____ , 18, _____

_____ , 12, _____

The number **after** 15 is _____ .

The number **before** 9 is _____ .

The number **before** 20 is _____ .

The number **before** 5 is _____ .

The number **after** 11 is _____ .

Name _____

Snowflake Sounds

Color by the code.

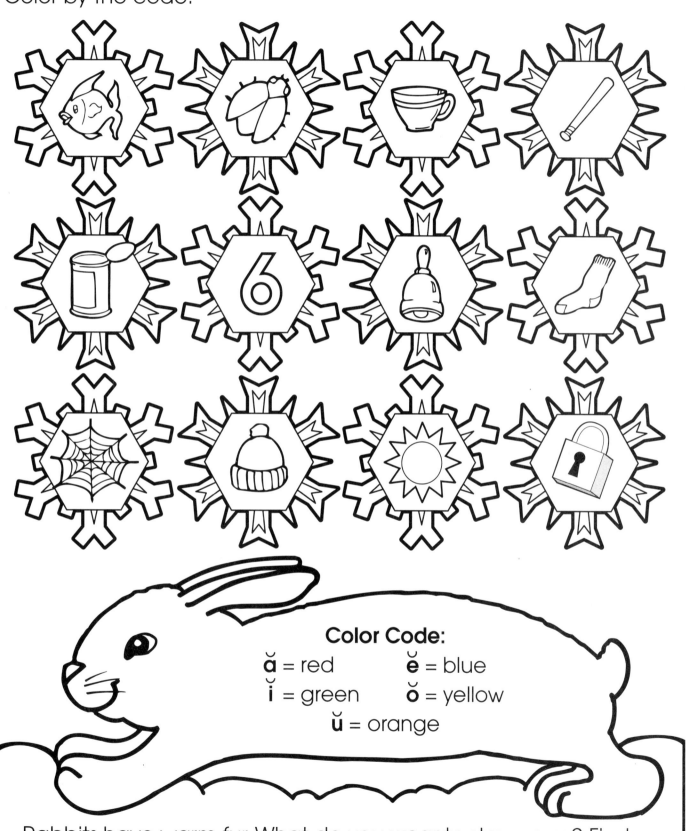

Color Code:

$\breve{a}$ = red $\breve{e}$ = blue

$\breve{i}$ = green $\breve{o}$ = yellow

$\breve{u}$ = orange

Rabbits have warm fur. What do you **wear** to stay warm? Find something above that you wear in winter. Circle that snowflake.

All Snuggled In

Write **a, e, i, o,** or **u** to finish each word.

Write the words in ABC order.

1. _____   5. _____

2. _____   6. _____

3. _____   7. _____

4. _____   8. _____

National Game And Puzzle Week

It's fun for all and all for fun during National Game and Puzzle Week, recognized annually during the last week in November. This "fun-tastic" week is the perfect time to add an entertaining twist to your lesson plans using this selection of great games and appealing puzzles.

Simon Says, "Have Fun!"

When it comes to listening skills, students are all ears for Simon! Use this simple direction-following game to help reinforce a variety of skills. Simon says…

- hold up your fingers to show the answer to 3 + 2.
- point to the part of your body that gives you the sense of hearing.
- raise your left foot.
- make a circle with your hands.
- write the letter to show the ending sound in *frog*.
- stand by something that begins with the letter *d*.

Expand on items like these, or try a few of your own. Your students will have so much fun, they won't even know they've been practicing basic skills!

Join The Lineup!

There's nothing fun about having your students line up at the door…or is there? This quick questioning game will have students eager to take their places in line. A few minutes before the class needs to leave the classroom, announce a category. Each student must name something that fits the category before she can join the line. Some skill-reinforcing topics include:

- types of transportation
- words that begin with the *sl* blend
- addition facts that equal ten
- words with short *o* sounds
- farm animals
- things that are hot
- winter activities
- foods in the fruits and vegetables group

Addition Fishin'

Add.
Find each sum in the pond.
Write.
Color each fish after you write its word.

Across

1. 0 + 1 = ___

3. 6 + 4 = ___

4. 3 + 5 = ___

6. 2 + 2 = ___

7. 3 + 4 = ___

Down

2. 6 + 3 = ___

3. 1 + 1 = ___

5. 2 + 1 = ___

6. 3 + 2 = ___

7. 3 + 3 = ___

Name _____

What's Hiding?

There's something in the box!
What could it be?
Solve the puzzle to find out.
Subtract.

$$\begin{array}{r} 10 \\ -\ 1 \\ \hline \end{array}$$
U

$$\begin{array}{r} 8 \\ -\ 5 \\ \hline \end{array}$$
K

$$\begin{array}{r} 10 \\ -\ 3 \\ \hline \end{array}$$
A

$$\begin{array}{r} 9 \\ -\ 7 \\ \hline \end{array}$$
M

$$\begin{array}{r} 10 \\ -\ 9 \\ \hline \end{array}$$
S

$$\begin{array}{r} 9 \\ -\ 9 \\ \hline \end{array}$$
R

$$\begin{array}{r} 10 \\ -\ 5 \\ \hline \end{array}$$
O

$$\begin{array}{r} 8 \\ -\ 2 \\ \hline \end{array}$$
F

$$\begin{array}{r} 8 \\ -\ 4 \\ \hline \end{array}$$
D

$$\begin{array}{r} 10 \\ -\ 2 \\ \hline \end{array}$$
E

Write the letter to match each answer.

___ ___ ___ ___ ___ ___
 7   2   5   9   1   8

What's For Dinner?

The cats are hungry.
They are looking for food.
Use the code to see what they will eat.

● □ ▭ ■ ➡   - - - - - - - - - - - - - - - -

○ ◇ △ 🐟   - - - - - - - - - - - - - - - -

☆ ▭ ◈ ♡   - - - - - - - - - - - - - - - -

△ ◇ ○ ◈   - - - - - - - - - - - - - - - -

◈ ○ ☾ ⊠   - - - - - - - - - - - - - - - -

✿ ☾ 🐟 ◈   - - - - - - - - - - - - - - - -

✿ ▭ ☾ ◈   - - - - - - - - - - - - - - - -

🐟	☾	☆	♡	▭	➡	■
a	e	f	h	i	k	l
●	△	✿	◈	○	◇	⊠
m	n	p	s	t	u	w

Name _____

Cat In The Box

Listen and do.

Note To The Teacher: Give each pair of students one copy of this page. In turn, have each player draw a horizontal or vertical line to connect two dots. If a player's line completes a square, ask him to write his initials in the box. If he boxes a cat, have him write his initials in the box twice. When the game ends, the player with the most sets of initials on the board is the winner.

Answer Keys

Page 32

8 − 2 = **6**   7 − 4 = **3**   6 − 3 = **3**

5 − 3 = **2**   8 − 5 = **3**   5 − 4 = **1**

6 − 2 = **4**   7 − 6 = **1**

8 − 6 = **2**   6 − 4 = **2**

Bonus Box: There were 8 apples in the basket. Sam used 3 apples to make a pie. How many apples were left in the basket?   **8−3 = 5**

Page 45

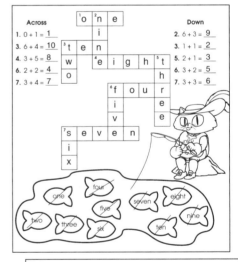

$\begin{array}{r}10\\-8\\\hline 2\end{array}$ (red)	$\begin{array}{r}8\\-5\\\hline 3\end{array}$ (blue)	$\begin{array}{r}10\\-4\\\hline 6\end{array}$ (green)	$\begin{array}{r}9\\-4\\\hline 5\end{array}$ (purple)
$\begin{array}{r}7\\-6\\\hline 1\end{array}$ (yellow)	$\begin{array}{r}9\\-5\\\hline 4\end{array}$ (orange)	$\begin{array}{r}10\\-5\\\hline 5\end{array}$ (purple)	$\begin{array}{r}8\\-4\\\hline 4\end{array}$ (orange)
$\begin{array}{r}7\\-5\\\hline 2\end{array}$ (red)	$\begin{array}{r}9\\-3\\\hline 6\end{array}$ (green)	$\begin{array}{r}8\\-6\\\hline 2\end{array}$ (red)	$\begin{array}{r}10\\-7\\\hline 3\end{array}$ (blue)
$\begin{array}{r}7\\-4\\\hline 3\end{array}$ (blue)	$\begin{array}{r}10\\-6\\\hline 4\end{array}$ (orange)	$\begin{array}{r}9\\-7\\\hline 2\end{array}$ (red)	$\begin{array}{r}8\\-7\\\hline 1\end{array}$ (yellow)

Page 33
- Bear
- Eagle
- Frog
- Owl
- Snake
- Whale

Page 58
1. bed
2. cup
3. dog
4. hat
5. pen
6. six
7. top
8. wig

Page 62
- milk
- tuna
- fish
- nuts
- stew
- peas
- pies

Page 36

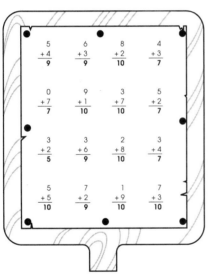

$\begin{array}{r}5\\+4\\\hline 9\end{array}$ $\begin{array}{r}6\\+3\\\hline 9\end{array}$ $\begin{array}{r}8\\+2\\\hline 10\end{array}$ $\begin{array}{r}4\\+3\\\hline 7\end{array}$

$\begin{array}{r}0\\+7\\\hline 7\end{array}$ $\begin{array}{r}9\\+1\\\hline 10\end{array}$ $\begin{array}{r}3\\+7\\\hline 10\end{array}$ $\begin{array}{r}5\\+2\\\hline 7\end{array}$

$\begin{array}{r}3\\+2\\\hline 5\end{array}$ $\begin{array}{r}3\\+6\\\hline 9\end{array}$ $\begin{array}{r}2\\+8\\\hline 10\end{array}$ $\begin{array}{r}3\\+4\\\hline 7\end{array}$

$\begin{array}{r}5\\+5\\\hline 10\end{array}$ $\begin{array}{r}7\\+2\\\hline 9\end{array}$ $\begin{array}{r}1\\+9\\\hline 10\end{array}$ $\begin{array}{r}7\\+3\\\hline 10\end{array}$

Page 60

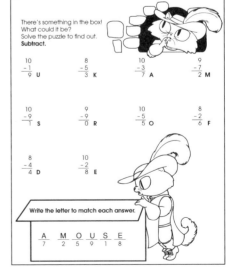

Across
1. 0 + 1 = 1
3. 6 + 4 = 10
4. 3 + 5 = 8
6. 2 + 2 = 4
7. 3 + 4 = 7

Down
2. 6 + 3 = 9
3. 1 + 1 = 2
5. 2 + 1 = 3
6. 3 + 2 = 5
7. 3 + 3 = 6

Crossword: one, ten, eight, four, three, seven, six, two, five, nine

Page 41

A Pioneer Picture Story

These pioneers rode in a [wagon] on their trip west.

The wagon was pulled by [oxen].

They loaded the wagon with [food].

They also brought [furniture].

They drove through tall [grass] and over [mountains].

Sometimes the pioneers were [sad]. It was hard work to go so far.

When they got to their new home they built a [house].

Page 61

There's something in the box! What could it be? Solve the puzzle to find out. **Subtract.**

$\begin{array}{r}10\\-1\\\hline 9\end{array}$ U $\begin{array}{r}8\\-5\\\hline 3\end{array}$ K $\begin{array}{r}10\\-3\\\hline 7\end{array}$ A $\begin{array}{r}9\\-7\\\hline 2\end{array}$ M

$\begin{array}{r}10\\-9\\\hline 1\end{array}$ S $\begin{array}{r}9\\-9\\\hline 0\end{array}$ R $\begin{array}{r}10\\-5\\\hline 5\end{array}$ O $\begin{array}{r}8\\-2\\\hline 6\end{array}$ F

$\begin{array}{r}8\\-4\\\hline 4\end{array}$ D $\begin{array}{r}10\\-2\\\hline 8\end{array}$ E

Write the letter to match each answer.

A M O U S E
7 2 5 9 1 8